RAILROADS OF WYOMING

Mike Danneman

First published 2021

Amberley Publishing
The Hill, Stroud
Gloucestershire, GL5 4EP

www.amberley-books.com

ISBN 978 1 4456 7694 4 (print)
ISBN 978 1 4456 7695 1 (ebook)

British Library Cataloguing in Publication Data.
A catalogue record for this book is available from the British Library.

Typesetting by SJmagic DESIGN SERVICES, India.
Printed in the UK.

Introduction

The territory that later became known as Wyoming featured mountains and rangelands in the western portion, with high elevation prairies called High Plains to the east. This unique topography caused Wyoming to be drier and windier in comparison to most of the United States, with greater temperature extremes because of this topography. Native Americans living here were nomadic tribes known as the Plains Indians.

One of the first known explorers of Wyoming was John Colter in 1807. While exploring the Rocky Mountains, he discovered towering waterfalls and steaming geysers in a region that would later be known as Yellowstone. In 1850, Jim Bridger located what is now known as Bridger Pass, which the Union Pacific later used in 1868. Bridger also explored Yellowstone and filed reports on the region that, like those of Colter, were largely disregarded as fictional.

Gold and rich farming land on the west coast lured many easterners through Wyoming as wagon trains slowly rolled over the Oregon Trail. Fort Laramie, located in south-eastern Wyoming, became an important station for the Pony Express and Overland stagecoaches, as well as a vital military post in the wars with the Plains Indians.

By the time President Abraham Lincoln signed the Pacific Railroad Act in July 1862, the nation was ready to open a vast interior for development and a desire for a transcontinental railroad to link the coasts. Union Pacific's forge west from Omaha, Nebraska, began in December 1863, finally steaming into Cheyenne on 13 November 1867, causing the region's population to balloon. Dubbed 'The Magic City of the Plains', Cheyenne grew from 400 inhabitants to more than 4,000 between August and December 1867.

The railroad built west over Sherman Hill, reaching Laramie on 4 May 1868. No longer experiencing Indian troubles, UP quickly pushed the railroad west to the Utah border at Wahsatch by the end of the year. The transcontinental railroad was completed with the golden spike, joining UP with Central Pacific at Promontory, Utah, on 10 May 1869. With Denver left off the transcontinental line, the Denver Pacific was quickly constructed from Denver to Cheyenne in 1870. The coming of the railroad brought economic opportunities for settlers to stay and live in Wyoming, instead of just traveling through to more hospitable climes further west. Government-sponsored expeditions to Yellowstone country found that reports by Colter and Bridger were true, and the incredible geothermal features, wildlife and scenery of the region became the world's first national park in 1872.

To reach the Pacific Northwest, Union Pacific predecessor Oregon Short Line Railway built a line to Montpelier, Idaho, from Granger, completed in August 1882. An early predecessor of Chicago & North Western entered eastern Wyoming through Douglas, building to Casper in 1886–88. This 'incursion' into UP's dominion prompted the building of the Cheyenne & Northern Railway to Wendover. UP took over the line in 1887, extending it to Orin Junction.

By the time Wyoming became the forty-fourth state of the union on 27 March 1890, the open-range cattle industry and the building of towns marked the end of the wild, western frontier. Where great herds of buffalo once grazed on the rolling landscape of Wyoming, a man named William F. 'Buffalo Bill' Cody now gave audiences a brief glimpse of cowboys, Indians and a way of life once seen in Wyoming's earlier days. At the turn of the century, he even took his Wild West Show to Great Britain and the European continent to share the west he loved.

While Union Pacific stimulated the economy of Wyoming's territorial era, after statehood in 1890, the Chicago, Burlington & Quincy began driving growth in the northern portion of the state. In November 1889, CB&Q entered Wyoming to Newcastle, constructing a line to Donkey Town (Gillette) by August 1891, extending the line through Sheridan in 1892, and finally connected to the Northern Pacific at Huntley, Montana, on 28 October 1894.

In 1893, UP went into receivership, with the Cheyenne & Northern route eventually going to the newly formed Colorado & Southern in 1898. CB&Q built west into Guernsey in 1900, and constructed a 131-mile branch line to the town of Cody, named after famous Buffalo Bill. During 1905–07, CB&Q built a line south of Frannie through Greybull, to Kirby. CB&Q bought control of C&S in 1908, and built south of Kirby through rugged Wind River Canyon, reaching Casper on 20 October 1913. New construction ceased after a new cutoff through Wendover Canyon between Guernsey and Wendover was completed in 1915.

As the twentieth century marched on, freight and passenger trains polished the rails of Wyoming routes as towns and industries grew. Union Pacific's main line route featured an abundance of tonnage and streamliners. CB&Q's routes weren't quite as busy, but managed to make a presence in the northern part of the state. Union Pacific developed some incredible steam locomotives to conquer the Wahsatch grade to Evanston, with Challenger and Big Boy articulated locomotives the epitome of modern steam locomotion. Both railroads modernised and converted to diesel power in the 1950s. CB&Q was merged with three other railroads to form Burlington Northern in 1970 and passenger service was transferred to Amtrak in 1971, but only on the UP main line.

For Wyoming railroading, the biggest revolution was right on the horizon. Thick seams of coal could be found under the rolling high plains of north-eastern Wyoming in Powder River Basin. Mines around Gillette began shipping via the newly formed BN on spurs built to reach them by 1972. BN began building a new line from Gillette to Orin to eventually access at least fifteen new coal mines that would help meet the country's growing need for low-cost, cleaner-burning low-sulphur coal.

Construction was delayed until 1976, and Chicago & North Western was granted to build the line jointly with BN, but financial issues caused the BN to forge ahead with the line on its own, completing it on 6 October 1979. The 116-mile Orin Line was the longest stretch of new railroad built in the U. S. since 1931. With UP financial backing, C&NW would later buy into the Orin Line.

Changes continued as Amtrak no longer serves the state of Wyoming, now using a scenic route through Colorado. BN merged with Atchison, Topeka & Santa Fe to become Burlington Northern Santa Fe in 1995, and C&NW was merged into Union Pacific in the same year. UP and BNSF own most of today's Wyoming railroad routes at 1,839 miles. Terminal and short line railroads operate the additional 49 miles of trackage. Wyoming railroading may not have the variety of other western states, but it ranks high in tonnage and scenery.

Join me for a visual outing of the railroads of Wyoming, through a selection of photographs that I have taken over the last thirty-six years. We begin the trip following the UP main line across the southern part of the state, including the route over Sherman Hill. Then we'll follow the the old C&S line north of Cheyenne and into beautiful Wendover Canyon, before launching on a tour of the former CB&Q main lines, now operated by BNSF. We'll finish off with a look at the Orin Line in Powder River Basin. I hope you enjoy this glimpse at the railroads of Wyoming!

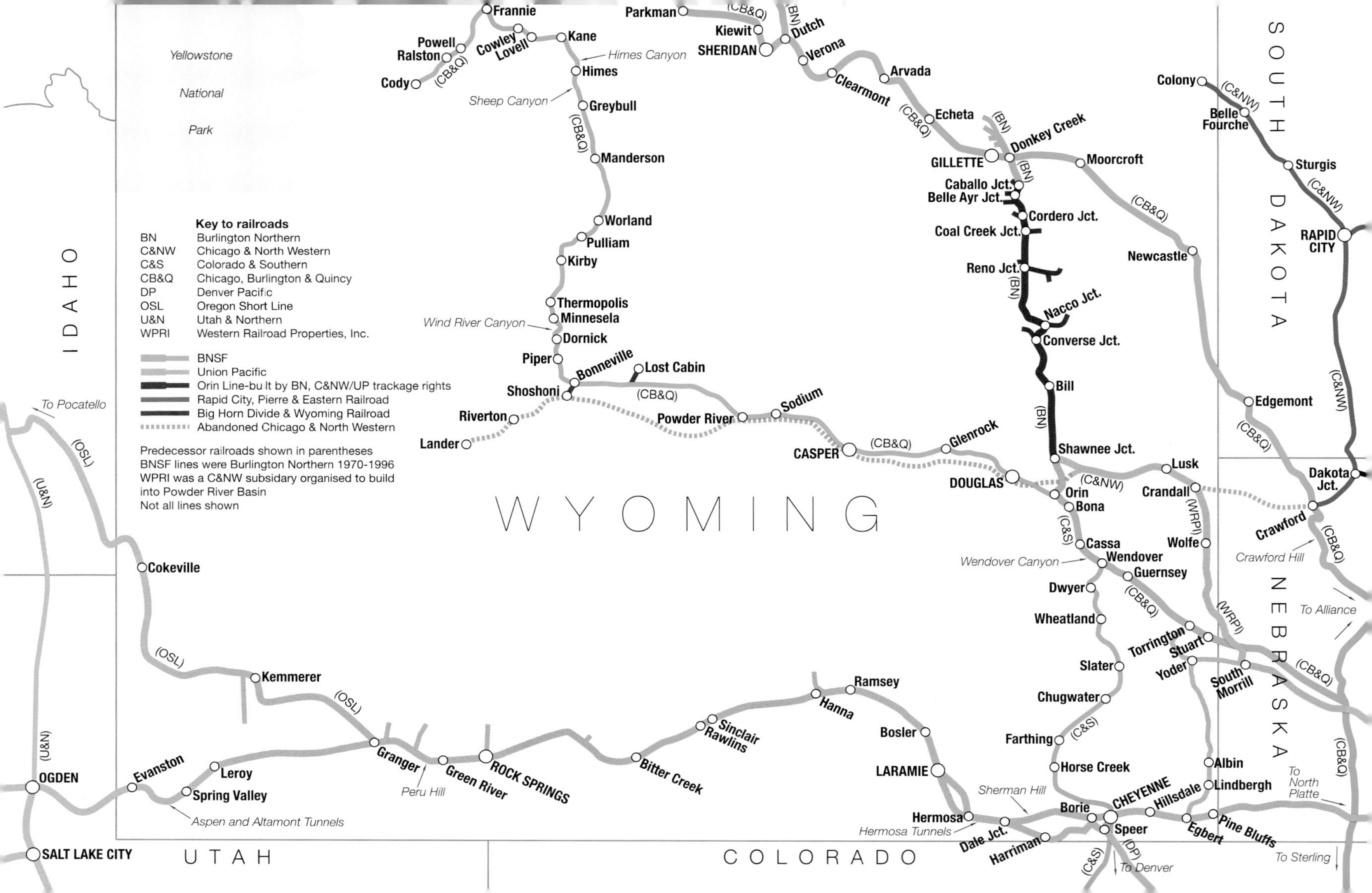

Key to railroads
BN Burlington Northern
C&NW Chicago & North Western
C&S Colorado & Southern
CB&Q Chicago, Burlington & Quincy
DP Denver Pacific
OSL Oregon Short Line
U&N Utah & Northern
WPRI Western Railroad Properties, Inc.
BNSF
Union Pacific
Orin Line-built by BN, C&NW/UP trackage rights
Rapid City, Pierre & Eastern Railroad
Big Horn Divide & Wyoming Railroad
Abandoned Chicago & North Western
Predecessor railroads shown in parentheses
BNSF lines were Burlington Northern 1970-1996
WPRI was a C&NW subsidary organised to build
into Powder River Basin
Not all lines shown
WYOMING
IDAHO
UTAH
COLORADO
NEBRASKA
SOUTH DAKOTA
Yellowstone National Park
Frannie
Powell
Ralston
Cody
Cowley
Lovell
Kane
Himes Canyon
Himes
Sheep Canyon
Greybull
Manderson
Worland
Pulliam
Kirby
Thermopolis
Minnesela
Wind River Canyon
Dornick
Piper
Bonneville
Lost Cabin
Shoshoni
Riverton
Lander
Powder River
Sodium
CASPER
Glenrock
DOUGLAS
Parkman
Kiewit
SHERIDAN
Dutch
Verona
Clearmont
Arvada
Echeta
Donkey Creek
GILLETTE
Moorcroft
Caballo Jct.
Belle Ayr Jct.
Cordero Jct.
Coal Creek Jct.
Reno Jct.
Nacco Jct.
Converse Jct.
Bill
Shawnee Jct.
Newcastle
Colony
Belle Fourche
Sturgis
RAPID CITY
Edgemont
Dakota Jct.
Crawford
Crawford Hill
Lusk
Crandall
Orin
Bona
Cassa
Wolfe
Wendover Canyon
Wendover
Guernsey
Dwyer
Wheatland
Torrington
Stuart
Yoder
South Morrill
To Alliance
Slater
Chugwater
Farthing
Horse Creek
Albin
Lindbergh
To North Platte
Sherman Hill
Borie
CHEYENNE
Hillsdale
Egbert
Pine Bluffs
Speer
To Sterling
To Denver
Hermosa
Hermosa Tunnels
Dale Jct.
Harriman
LARAMIE
Bosler
Ramsey
Hanna
Sinclair
Rawlins
Bitter Creek
ROCK SPRINGS
Green River
Granger
Peru Hill
Kemmerer
Cokeville
To Pocatello
Leroy
Evanston
Spring Valley
Aspen and Altamont Tunnels
OGDEN
SALT LAKE CITY
(BN)
(C&NW)
(C&S)
(CB&Q)
(DP)
(OSL)
(U&N)
(WRPI)

Passing milepost 107 on the Colorado & Southern line that treks south to Denver, a Burlington Northern coal train crosses the Wyoming state line into Colorado on 5 July 1989.

Union Pacific Challenger No. 3985 rolls west just east of Pine Bluffs on the railroad's Sidney Subdivision on 9 October 2008. The big four-cylinder simple articulated locomotive was built in 1943 and restored by UP employees between 1979 and 1981, spending many years serving alongside never-retired Northern No. 844 in the railroad's steam program.

Union Pacific No. 3985 approaches Egbert on a blustery 9 October 2008. The huge 4-6-6-4 articulated locomotive is operating westbound on the Sidney Subdivision, returning to her home base of Cheyenne.

Sunrise on the Union Pacific main line east of Hillsdale silhouettes a westbound freight headed for a crew change at the division point of Cheyenne on the morning of 26 March 2008.

A Union Pacific freight climbs Archer Hill east of Cheyenne on 26 March 2008. UP GE ES44AC No. 5270 and EMD SD60M No. 2474 power the eastbound train toward North Platte, Nebraska.

Union Pacific 4-6-6-4 Challenger No. 3985 thunders westbound on the approach to the top of Archer Hill on 9 October 2008. Fireman Ed Dickens can be seen in the cab – Ed has been UP's Manager of Heritage Equipment & Facilities since 2011.

With Engineer Steve Lee at the throttle, Union Pacific Challenger No. 3985 storms up Archer Hill east of Cheyenne on the morning of 23 September 2003.

A westbound Union Pacific freight has stopped in front of the depot at Cheyenne waiting for a fresh crew as the old crew steps off lead locomotive EMD SD40-2 No. 3718 and heads for the station on a warm July afternoon in 1984.

Basking in the sun on the Cheyenne turntable is Union Pacific Northern No. 838, along with EMD SW10 switcher No. 96, on 8 October 2008. Over the years, the 4-8-4 has donated many parts to keep sister steam locomotive No. 844 operable.

Inside the Cheyenne roundhouse on 25 March 2013, Union Pacific's two EMD E9As wait for another opportunity to pull the railroad's passenger trains. Both were built in 1955, and in the early 1990s UP sent them to VMV Enterprises in Paducah, Kentucky, to be remanufactured.

After changing crews, an eastbound Union Pacific double-stack train of APL (American President Lines) containers departs Cheyenne on 17 May 1991. The gold-leaf dome of Wyoming's state capitol building can be seen in the background in downtown Cheyenne.

EMD DDA40X No. 6923 leads a westbound freight, heavy with stock cars on the head end, out of Cheyenne in April 1984. This group of big twin-diesel locomotives were numbered in the 6900 series and were nicknamed 'Centennials', since they was constructed 100 years after the completion of the transcontinental railroad on 10 May 1869.

With stormy skies building over Cheyenne, a westbound Union Pacific freight heads for Speer on Track 3 for a trip over Sherman Hill on the afternoon of 25 May 2011.

A westbound Union Pacific freight curves toward Borie at milepost 518 on Track 1 following the original alignment over Sherman Hill. The stark snow-covered scenery doesn't divulge that the date is 29 April 2019, and it should be springtime!

A trio of GE ES44AC locomotives power a Union Pacific coal train climbing toward Speer on the morning of 4 May 2019. The train will divert from the Sherman Hill grade at Speer and head south on the railroad's Greeley Subdivision toward Denver, Colorado.

The 46-mile Harriman Cutoff over Sherman Hill was completed in 1953 and reduced the ruling grade from 1.55 per cent occurring on Tracks 1 and 2, to 0.82 per cent for this line, also known as Track 3. Heavy westbound steam-powered trains would take this route and facilities were built to support these locomotives. A westbound UP freight passes a water tank that still survives at the location of Harriman on 14 April 2007.

On the beautiful early autumn day of 24 September 2003, an eastbound Union Pacific freight crests the summit of Sherman Hill at Sherman. When built in 1867, the station of Sherman was the highest railroad station in the world, named in honor of Civil War General William Tecumseh Sherman, who also happened to be the tallest general in the U. S. Army.

A pair of GE C40-8 locomotives power an eastbound Union Pacific manifest freight through the sweeping curves approaching the summit of Sherman Hill on 24 September 2003.

Led by EMD SD40-2 No. 3391, an eastbound Union Pacific double-stack train notches it up as it curves out of Dale Junction and heads for Dale on Sherman Hill's Track 1 in July 1984.

Approaching Dale Junction, a westbound Union Pacific 'K-Line' stack train, loaded with bright red containers, passes by the unique rock formations at Dale while crossing Sherman Hill on 16 October 2007.

Westbound on Sherman Hill's Track 1, a Union Pacific double-stack is now rolling downgrade at Dale on a pleasant 17 September 2008. The train will soon be joined by Track 3 of the Harriman Cutoff at Dale Junction.

An eastbound Union Pacific unit potash train cruises by Dale Junction over Track 1 on 17 September 2008. The rear of the train is at the actual junction with Track 3, seen curving off to the left, built as a low-grade line in 1952–53 as an alternate westward main over the hill.

A pair of brand-new General Electric ES44AC locomotives, Nos 7651 and 7653, power an eastbound Union Pacific freight on Track 1 at Dale Junction while negotiating Sherman Hill on the morning of 16 October 2007.

A westbound Union Pacific grain train waits for traffic to pass as the caboose of an eastbound intermodal train zips by at Dale Junction in July 1984. The train will soon depart, all four EMD SD40-2s working hard to get the heavy unit train rolling into Hermosa Tunnels.

Three Union Pacific GE AC4400CW-CTE locomotives bring a heavy westbound unit train up toward the Hermosa Tunnels between Dale Junction and Hermosa on 29 October 2008.

An eastbound Union Pacific grain train thunders out of the northern bore of the Hermosa Tunnels on the climb up Sherman Hill just east of Hermosa on 25 September 2003. This line change through Hermosa was put in service in 1901, with the second tunnel drilled through on 14 October 1918, making the entire route over Sherman Hill double-track.

Union Pacific EMD SD70M No. 5000 leads an eastbound freight out of the northern bore of the Hermosa Tunnels on Track 1 between Hermosa and Dale Junction on 25 September 2003.

An eastbound Union Pacific freight approaches the Hermosa Tunnels leaving Hermosa in July 1984. EMD's SD40-2 ruled the UP main line in this era, and the power on this train is no exception, led by No. 3280.

On 25 September 2003, an eastbound Union Pacific stack train enters the cut approaching the twin Hermosa Tunnels at Hermosa. Trailing lead UP EMD SD70M No. 4363 is a pair of General Electric locomotives from eastern U. S. railroads' Norfolk Southern and CSX.

A westbound Union Pacific potash train emerges from the northern bore on Track 1 of the 1,828-foot Hermosa Tunnels on UP's Sherman Hill crossing on the Laramie Subdivision in Wyoming on 29 October 2008.

With stormy weather moving east, a westbound Union Pacific unit grain train curves through the rocky cut exiting Hermosa Tunnels at Hermosa on 25 March 2008.

Wyoming's Medicine Bow Mountains disappear into the haze of a western horizon as an eastbound Union Pacific freight passes underneath the signal bridge at Hermosa on 12 September 2007.

Led by EMD SD70M No. 4742, GE C44-9W No. 9513 and GE AC4400CW No. 7291, an eastbound Union Pacific intermodal train passes milepost 550 west of Hermosa. The train is climbing Sherman Hill on Track 1 on the afternoon of 24 September 2003.

Union Pacific EMD SD90MAC-H No. 8930 leads an eastbound freight through downtown Laramie. Businesses in the old historic buildings lining First Street appear busy on 14 of September 2006.

In very much spring-like weather for Wyoming, with threatening clouds and a dusting of snow, an eastbound Union Pacific freight approaches Laramie in April 1984. On the point is the world's largest diesel locomotive, the DDA40X 'Centennial'. At almost 100 feet long and 6,600 hp, only UP had them, and a few came out of storage one last time in 1984 and early '85 during an increase of traffic.

Two miles east of Bosler on UP's Laramie Subdivision, an eastbound Union Pacific K-Line stack train cruises past milepost 580 led by new GE ES44AC No. 5329 on 14 September 2006.

Union Pacific EMD SD40-2 No. 3743 leads a freight past the signals at mile 634.6 between Como and Ramsey on 5 July 1988. Just barely visible above the train in the background is another westbound on Track 2 that is overtaking the slower freight train.

Union Pacific Big Boy No. 4014 steams westbound past the signals at mile 634.6 between Como and Ramsey on 4 May 2019. The passenger train is headed to Utah, in 'The Great Race to Ogden' for a 150th anniversary celebration of the completion of the transcontinental railroad and Golden Spike. UP restored this giant 4-8-8-4 articulated locomotive just in time for this special event.

A westbound Union Pacific double-stack intermodal train cruises through Sinclair, 7 miles east of the division point and crew change of Rawlins, on the afternoon of 4 May 2019.

Spectators are beginning to gather with the arrival of Union Pacific Big Boy No. 4014, as freight trains continued to polish the main line through Rawlins, on the cool afternoon of 6 May 2019.

The sun is slowly sinking into the western horizon and reflects off the rails and approaching eastbound Union Pacific freight at West Rawlins on a brilliant 8 February 2007.

A pair of Union Pacific GE AC4400CWs haul an eastbound freight past a trackside waterhole at the high-desert location of Riner, 17 miles west of Rawlins, on 5 May 2019.

Union Pacific Big Boy No. 4014 passes skeletal remains of a steam locomotive servicing facility located at remote Bitter Creek on 5 May 2019. The special passenger train is headed to a celebration in Ogden, Utah, for the 150th anniversary celebration of the completion of the transcontinental railroad and Golden Spike.

Six General Electric locomotives, led by C36-7 No. 9005, rumbles eastbound around a curve just east of Green River on the clear summer day of 6 July 1988.

Just moments after changing crews, a westbound Union Pacific intermodal train departs the division point of Green River on the afternoon of 10 March 2004. The stately red-brick depot built in 1910, fronted by a 40-foot-long colonnade and arched entrance ways, is second in size in Wyoming only to the depot in Cheyenne.

Two sets of Union Pacific EMD SD40-2s rest on the night of 19 January 2013, at Green River. These older 3,000-hp locomotives are used for switching the yard here, while three bigger GE locomotives behind the No. 3203 set will later be used to power a unit soda ash train.

A westbound Union Pacific double-stack train heads up Peru Hill west of Green River late in the afternoon of 9 October 2015. The main line here takes the railroad upgrade away from the Green River toward Granger.

Traffic on the road is very quiet this morning, unlike the parallel Union Pacific main line, which is humming with trains. As seen from inside a long-abandoned gas station along the old Lincoln Highway at James Town, a UP unit oil train climbs Peru Hill on the morning of 13 March 2012. The skeletons of no-longer-needed gas pumps still stand out front, waiting for customers that will never come.

An eastbound Union Pacific freight descends Peru Hill, west of Green River, during the last light of 12 March 2012. Making some interesting patterns, the first few cars on the train are wrapped lumber loads on center beam flatcars.

The setting sun lights up a passing thunderstorm, as ambient light from a brilliant Wyoming sky illuminates an empty potash train powered by a trio of Union Pacific EMD SD40-2s climbing Peru Hill, west of Green River, on 5 July 1988.

Union Pacific Big Boy No. 4014 and Northern No. 844 power a westbound passenger special into Granger at 6:21 a.m. on 6 May 2019. Steam exhaust condenses in the icy cold temperature on this beautiful morning, forging a spectacular sight.

One of Union Pacific's specially painted 'heritage' locomotives, this one honoring the Chicago & North Western, leads an eastbound stack train over the old highway bridge at Ragan between Spring Valley and Leroy on the railroad's Evanston Subdivision on 7 May 2019.

Climbing the grade toward the Altamont Tunnel, Union Pacific Big Boy No. 4014 is double-headed with Northern No. 844, leading the passenger special to 150th anniversary of the Golden Spike at Ragan between Leroy and Spring Valley on 6 May 2019.

An eastbound Union Pacific freight drops downgrade just east of Spring Valley on the morning of 7 May 2019. Just west of this location, the Aspen Tunnel was a single-track bottleneck for many years, until completion of a second tunnel (Altamont) in 1949 created a double-track main line for the railroad its entire distance between Council Bluffs, Iowa and Salt Lake City, Utah.

Union Pacific's articulated Big Boy No. 4014 stands across from the local power tied up in the yard at Evanston on the afternoon of 6 May 2019. The Big Boy is leading a train to Ogden, Utah, for a celebration of the 150th anniversary of the completion of the transcontinental railroad.

On a cold and snowy winter day on Union Pacific's Pocatello Subdivision, an eastbound stack train speeds by east of Cokeville on 20 January 2013. The train is passing by Cokeville Meadows National Wildlife Refuge at a siding location named Pixley.

A northbound Burlington Northern Santa Fe freight rumbles over the truss bridge spanning Union Pacific's busy main line at Cheyenne on 4 July 1999. This is BNSF's Front Range Subdivision from Denver, Colorado, to Wendover, and is a former Colorado & Southern route.

Crossing a wood trestle south of Farthing is a southbound Burlington Northern Santa Fe coal train as it approaches Altus on the former Colorado & Southern main line between Cheyenne and Wendover on 4 July 1999.

On the afternoon of 30 May 1998, a southbound Burlington Northern Santa Fe freight arrives at Chugwater. The train is powered by a pair of EMD locomotives, former Santa Fe SD45-2 No. 6513 and BN SD40-2 No. 7195.

A colorful locomotive powers a southbound BNSF freight at Slater on 30 May 1998, with Santa Fe C40-8W No. 870, Burlington Northern GE B30-7A No. 4056 and Santa Fe EMD GP7u No. 2096 leading the way.

It's bright and sunny on 30 May 1998, as a Burlington Northern Santa Fe freight heads northward through Slater. This route is the former Colorado & Southern between Cheyenne and Wendover, and powering the train are a Burlington Northern GE C30-7 and EMD SD40-2 duo.

A southbound Burlington Northern Santa Fe freight passes the old railroad station at Wheatland on 4 July 1999. The depot was built in 1895 serving as a focal point to the community until it closed in 1969. Ironically, after its listing in the National Register of Historic Places in 1996, the depot was torn down, probably not long after this photograph was taken.

A northbound BNSF coal train heads back to the Powder River Basin for loading as it traverses the grasslands around Dwyer on 3 May 2007. Today, a 4,660-foot siding exists here, with this location named for J. E. Dwyer, a superintendent of the Colorado & Southern.

On 30 May 1998, a Burlington Northern Santa Fe freight approaches the south siding switch of Dwyer. BN EMD SD40-2 No. 7002 and LRCX GE SF30C No. 9556 power the northbound train. LRCX No. 9556 is a rebuilt Santa Fe U36C in a lease locomotive fleet from Livingston Rebuild Center in Montana.

Kansas City Southern EMD SD60 No. 754 leads an eastbound Burlington Northern coal train through East Stuart on the BN's Valley Subdivision near the Nebraska state line on 25 July 1992.

Seven six-axle locomotives power a Burlington Northern empty coal train over the impressive 640-foot North Platte River Bridge at Guernsey on 4 July 1988. The train is headed west on the railroad's Canyon Subdivision.

With thunderstorms brewing to the east, a westbound Burlington Northern coal train is seen departing Guernsey on 4 July 1988. Behind lead BN EMD SD40-2 No. 7281 is a pair of run through locomotives from Santa Fe and Union Pacific.

A Burlington Northern Santa Fe coal train pops out of 3,334-foot Tunnel 1 just west of Guernsey on 7 July 1999. Note the heavy wood tunnel lining still being used to support the unstable rock and earth around the bore.

In the spring of 1998, BNSF daylighted Sunset Tunnel, also known as the 1,928-foot Tunnel 2 between Guernsey and Wendover. Besides the massive amount of work to remove the tunnel, BNSF also had to stabilize the soft earthen boundaries of the excavation with a concrete mixture sprayed to the sides of the cut, giving the scenery a strange new look. On 21 June 2019, an eastbound BNSF coal train heads through the huge cut.

Passing over Cottonwood Creek, a Burlington Northern Santa Fe coal train heads west through Wendover, passing an abandoned homestead and derelict GMC tow truck on 7 June 2002.

Powered by a trio of Burlington Northern EMD SD70MAC locomotives, an empty BNSF coal train snakes through scenic Wendover Canyon just west of Wendover on 25 May 1997.

A Burlington Northern Santa Fe loaded coal train in Powder River Basin is eastbound on the BNSF's Canyon Subdivision along the North Platte River in scenic Wendover Canyon east of Cassa on 9 July 1999.

On 5 July 1999, an eastbound Burlington Northern Santa Fe coal train rolls along the North Platte River in the splendid scenery of Wendover Canyon east of Cassa.

Five Cascade green Burlington Northern locomotives, three EMD SD40-2s and two GE C30-7s, power a BNSF coal train through Wendover Canyon east of Cassa on 9 July 1999. This remote location along the North Platte River is on the BNSF's Canyon Subdivision.

Toward the end of the day on 25 May 1997, a Burlington Northern Santa Fe empty coal train passes through the growing shadows of Wendover Canyon between Wendover and Cassa.

Approaching Cassa on the morning of 9 July 1999, a westbound Burlington Northern Santa Fe freight, with Boeing airline parts and fuselages cars up front, makes it way along the banks of the North Platte River and through a cut with a colorful locomotive consist leading the way.

Decked out in the 'Grinstein' paint scheme, named after a chairman of Burlington Northern, a trio of BN EMD SD70MACs lead an empty coal train westbound out of Wendover Canyon at Cassa on 9 July 1999.

The very last light of the day on 18 October 2018 softly paints a BNSF coal train curving westbound between Elkhorn and Bona. The railroad skirts Glendo Reservoir and Glendo State Park through this area.

A BNSF empty coal train rolls northward through Bona on the way to the Orin Line in Powder River Basin for another trainload of coal on the afternoon of 16 October 2018.

A Union Pacific excursion train dubbed the 'City of Yoder' ran from Cheyenne to South Morrill, Nebraska, and returned on the railroad's Yoder Subdivision on 10 July 2009, for the Union Pacific Historical Society. Here, the special smokes it up on the return trip at mile 215.3, a few miles east of Albin.

Union Pacific's A-B-A set of EMD E9 cab units power an eastbound passenger train past mile 231.5 west of Lindbergh on 10 July 2009. The classy train ran from Cheyenne to South Morrill, Nebraska, and returned on the Yoder Subdivision for the UP Historical Society.

Union Pacific Challenger No. 3985 rattles an old grain elevated at Yoder on 23 September 2003, pulling a long passenger train eastbound toward South Morrill, Nebraska.

An eastbound coal train led by Chicago & North Western GE AC4400CW No. 8835 rumbles through Wolfe on the Union Pacific's Powder River Subdivision on 6 July 1996.

At sunset on 6 July 1996, an eastbound Union Pacific coal train leaves Lusk in the dust. Barely visible on the right is an old wooden water tower that still stands here from the days when it quenched the thirst of Chicago & North Western steam locomotives.

A Burlington Northern coal train led by five GE locomotives climbs out of a sag in the undulating Black Hills Subdivision main line west of Newcastle at Pedro on the afternoon of 3 July 1989.

Four C30-7s and a U30C team up to provide 15,000 hp of General Electric locomotion, dressed in Burlington Northern's Cascade green and black, as they pull an eastbound coal train just east of Newcastle on a hot 3 July 1989.

Three brand-new Burlington Northern EMD SD70MACs, painted in 'Grinstein' colors, lead a coal empty through Moorcroft early on the morning of 13 September 1995.

Burlington Northern GE C30-7 No. 5554 passes a sister locomotive on another coal empty on a siding just east of Donkey Creek on 29 May 1998. Empty coal trains are frequently staged here waiting to head south on the Orin Line for loading, when the mine is ready for them. Later, BNSF even built a new yard at this location for the same purpose.

As rain and thunderstorms roll eastward, three BNSF coal trains wait in the yard at Donkey Creek, on the Black Hills Subdivision east of Gillette, on the afternoon of 30 May 2009.

A bull of the bovine persuasion is about to cross Echeta Road as a pair of Burlington Northern SD40-2s hustle an eastbound 'Z' train past milepost 627 through Croton on the morning of 14 June 1997. Croton is located between the sidings of Lariat and Echeta on the BNSF's Big Horn Subdivision west of Gillette.

Passing the old water tank and grain elevators still located at the town of Arvada is a BNSF coal train heading west on BNSF's Big Horn Subdivision on 14 June 2014.

Running eastbound out of an approaching springtime storm, a BNSF intermodal train rolls toward Clearmont on the railroad's Big Horn Subdivision, on 14 June 2014.

A pair of former Burlington Northern EMD SD40-2s, Nos 7898 and 6372, pull an eastbound BNSF freight past a ranch east of Verona on 1 July 2002.

Surrounded by the verdant grasses of springtime is an eastbound coal train east of Verona on 14 June 1997. Powering the train loaded with Powder River Basin coal is Oakway Leasing EMD SD60 No. 9087, a Burlington Northern EMD SD40-2 and a pair of BN GE C30-7s.

A westbound BNSF coal empty rumbles through Dutch as rain moves east over the Big Horn Subdivision on 14 June 2014. In a mile or so, the train will head up the BNSF Dutch Subdivision for loading on one of the branch line's coal mines.

Not long after departing the crew change point of Sheridan, an eastbound Burlington Northern Santa Fe coal train aims for the morning sun west of Dutch on 1 July 2002.

Three Burlington Northern Santa Fe trains wait to depart the yard at Sheridan on 14 June 1997. The coal train led by BN EMD SD60M No. 9245 has yet to get a fresh crew, but the other two are ready to go. The intermodal train on the right, with leased LMX GE B39-8 No. 8516 leading, will depart first.

Burlington Northern EMD SD60M No. 9269 takes a spin on the turntable at Sheridan on the morning of 24 September 2002. This turntable is an unusual through truss design, whereas most tables are girder-type models. It is still used today as the BNSF yard at Sheridan has no wye and it's the only way to turn locomotives when needed.

An eastbound Burlington Northern Santa Fe freight rolls eastward through East Kiewit on 13 September 1999. The area north of Sheridan is rich with coal mining history, but one by one, the underground mines closed. In later years, a flood loader silo was built in 1966/7 to ship coal from the Acme mine, which became an open pit operation. Eventually the mine closed and shortly after this photo, the silo in the background was demolished.

A Burlington Northern Santa Fe coal train, powered by BNSF EMD SD60M No. 9227 and two Oakway Leasing EMD SD60s, heads west between Sheridan and Kiewit on 6 June 2002.

Under a threatening springtime sky, Burlington Northern EMD SD40-2 No. 6927 leads cabless GE B30-7A 'B unit' Nos 4038 and 4006 on an eastbound intermodal train at Parkman on 15 June 1997.

A southbound Burlington Northern freight approaches Douglas on the BN's Casper Subdivision on the morning of 12 May 1995. The empty grade in the background is the former Chicago & North Western line to Lander, nicknamed the 'Cowboy Line'.

A northbound Burlington Northern Santa Fe freight behind GE C44-9W No. 5223 waits for the arrival of an southbound powered by a pair of BN EMD SD60Ms and a green BNSF EMD SD40-2 at the crew change of Casper on 11 September 2002.

Northbound on the Burlington Northern Santa Fe's Casper Subdivision is a freight led by BNSF EMD SD40-2 No. 6338 at Sodium on 1 September 1998.

A northbound Burlington Northern Santa Fe freight rounds the wide curve through Powder River on BNSF's Casper Subdivision on 1 September 1998. Behind lead unit EMD SD40-2 No. 6338 is BNSF GP9u No. 1638 and Livingston Rebuild Center (LRCX) GE SF30C No. 9556, both former Santa Fe locomotives.

Bonneville Transloaders, Inc. owns the Bad Water Railway, which started out as the Bad Water Line based in Riverton and was established in 1995 after BTI bought 'Cowboy Line' trackage abandoned by the Chicago & North Western. In this view, BTI EMD SW1500 No. 1 pulls a small train west of Bonneville on 2 October 1997. This part of the trackage connects BNSF's Casper Subdivision trackage at milepost 304 at Bonneville to Shoshoni, with trackage west of Shoshoni now abandoned.

In May 2002, BTI was bought by Bighorn Divide & Wyoming Railroad, Inc. (BDW). On 22 June 2016, a southbound BNSF freight departs Bonneville as a BDW train powered by EMD GP38 No. 2001 and EMD SW1500 No. 1001 switch a large cut of cars in the yard.

Rolling southbound on the Casper Subdivision, a BNSF manifest freight crosses the bridge over Tough Creek just south of the siding at Piper on the afternoon of 3 July 2019.

A multicolor locomotive consist leads a northbound Burlington Northern Santa Fe freight into Wind River Canyon as it crosses the Wind River between Piper and Dornick on 8 July 1999. Powering the train is BNSF warbonnnet-clad C44-9W No. 793, former Santa Fe EMD SD40-2 No. 6902 and a former Milwaukee Road, now EMD leasing SD40-2.

A northbound Burlington Northern Santa Fe freight crosses the Wind River between Piper and Dornick sidings on 7 July 1999. The view is framed from inside an abandoned Chicago, Burlington & Quincy tunnel that once carried this main line into Wind River Canyon. This old alignment was relocated during the construction of Boysen Dam that began in 1946. Contractor Morrison-Knudsen Company built a 7,131-foot tunnel that actually ran under the dam and a portion of the reservoir. The new rail line opened in September 1950, with completion of the dam itself on 16 February 1952.

In scenic Wind River Canyon, a northbound BNSF freight exits Black Tunnel south of Dornick on 25 May 2011. Powered by warbonnet GE C44-9W No. 4706 and Union Pacific EMD SD70M No. 4274, the train has Boeing 737 fuselages headed for Washington state on the head end, and look to be a tight squeeze through the tunnel.

Burlington Northern EMD GP38-2 No. 2353 leads a southbound BNSF freight through Tunnel 2 in rugged Wind River Canyon just south of Dornick on 13 October 1997.

A northbound Burlington Northern Santa Fe freight rumbles through scenic Wind River Canyon at Dornick, Wyoming, on 2 October 1997. Leading the varicolored consist is BN EMD SD40-2 No. 8177, followed by Santa Fe GE C40-8W No. 901 and Montana Rail Link EMD F45 No. 390.

Outrunning a storm to the south of Wind River Canyon, a northbound BNSF freight slinks along the banks of a swollen Wind River on 20 June 2017. The train is approaching the north end of the scenic canyon between the sidings of Dornick and Minnesela on BNSF's Casper Subdivision.

A northbound BNSF freight escapes the rugged depths of Wind River Canyon as it passes the siding of Minnesela and approaches Thermopolis on the afternoon of 20 June 2017.

Led by EMD SD70ACe No. 9235, BNSF's Denver to Laurel freight passes through several rock cuts while pacing the Bighorn River at Thermopolis on 24 June 2018. In the background are some of the hot springs and other facilities of Wyoming's Hot Springs State Park.

A southbound BNSF freight approaches the town of Winchester between the sidings of Pulliam and Kirby on the BNSF's Casper Subdivision on the afternoon of 20 June 2017.

On a sunny 21 June 2017, a southbound BNSF double-stack train appears beneath the rocky cliffs of beautiful Sheep Canyon north of Greybull.

BNSF's Cowley turn follows the Bighorn River through remote and impressive Sheep Canyon as it passes milepost 414 while returning to Greybull on the sunny afternoon of 27 June 2018.

A pair of orange BNSF EMD SD70MACs power the Cowley turn through Sheep Canyon past milepost 414 out of Greybull on the morning of 23 June 2016.

The morning sun lights up the steep rock walls of Sheep Canyon on 22 June 2017, as a northbound BNSF manifest freight curves along the Bighorn River north of Greybull.

On BNSF's Casper Subdivision, a southbound manifest freight crosses a bridge between Himes and Spence on the afternoon of 25 June 2018.

BNSF's Cowley turn out of Greybull passes milepost 419 as the local freight skirts a pair of red buttes heading southbound between Himes and Spence on 3 July 2019.

On the morning of 25 June 2018, BNSF's Cowley turn passes through the rugged landscape north of Sheep Canyon as it approaches Himes on the scenic Casper Subdivision. The local freight will serve several industries between Himes and Cowley before returning home to Greybull.

A northbound BNSF freight passes through sharp curves entering Himes Canyon on 24 June 2017. This remote canyon is located along the Bighorn River between the sidings of Himes and Kane.

A southbound BNSF manifest freight follows the Bighorn River through stark Himes Canyon between Kane and Himes in a view from Scorpion Ridge on 25 June 2018. Hiking around on the sharp rocks in this rugged locale can tear up the soles on a new pair of boots!

BNSF's Cowley turn heads southbound through the fascinating topography of Himes Canyon, located between Himes and Kane, Wyoming, on 25 June 2018. The local train operates north out of Greybull on BNSF's Casper Subdivision.

A local freight led by Burlington Northern EMD GP15-1 No. 1390 is about to roll through a curve after crossing the bridge over the Shoshone River at Lovell on 2 September 1998.

On a cool 12 October 1997, a Burlington Northern Santa Fe freight passes the western shore of Bighorn Lake as it departs Kane. A trio of warbonnet-garbed GE locomotives power the northbound train, in various styles of BNSF and Santa Fe lettering.

Ten miles south of Lovell on BNSF's Casper Subdivision, is the siding of Kane. BNSF's Cowley turn that operates out of Greybull has just met a northbound freight at Kane and is now headed southbound past the mesas bordering the main line here on 23 June 2017. Leading the train is former Burlington Northern EMD SD60M No. 1410, still painted Cascade green, followed by newer EMD SD70MAC No. 8912.

Approaching Vocation, BNSF's Cody local is four cars and a caboose powered by two former Burlington Northern SD70MACs on the morning of 24 June 2016. Vocation was a siding and station just west of Ralston on the CB&Q's line to Cody near the Heart Mountain Relocation Center, a concentration camp used for internment of Japanese Americans evicted from mainly the West Coast Exclusion Zone during the Second World War. At one point, it had a peak population of over 10,000, making it the third-largest 'town' in Wyoming before it closed on 10 November 1945.

BNSF's Cody local crosses a wood trestle approaching Vocation, just west of Ralston, on 28 June 2018. Today's local has a large cut of covered hoppers up front to be set out at Ralston Elevator a few miles ahead.

On 28 June 2018, BNSF's Cody local sets out with a large cut of covered hoppers at Ralston Elevator. This branch line is 42.6 miles long, running from the Frannie on the Casper Subdivision to Cody.

BNSF's Cody local is eastbound west of Ralston on 24 June 2016. The local is crossing Bridge 29.14 over Eaglenest Creek with four cars and caboose. The town of Cody is a gateway to renowned Yellowstone National Park.

BNSF's Cody local rumbles eastward over a unique bridge arrangement while departing Ralston, Wyoming, on 28 June 2018. The local is passing over a combination girder bridge with wood trestle approaches, over an old highway overpass, which is all passing over Alkali Creek. The eastbound train is headed for a main line connection at Frannie, and is EMD-powered by GP38-3R No. 2392 and SD40-2 No. 1659, still in Burlington Northern Cascade green.

Trundling eastbound past milepost 14 on BNSF's branch to Cody is BNSF's Cody local heading for the Casper Subdivision main line at Frannie on 24 June 2016. Two former Burlington Northern EMD SD70MACs power the short train of four cars and a BN caboose. This branch line is the last of its kind on BNSF in Wyoming – all the other branches are coal-only spurs around Powder River Basin.

An eastbound Burlington Northern coal train led by GE C30-7 No. 5109 exits Powder River Basin as it rolls through Donkey Creek Junction east of Gillette on 6 July 1994. The train is leaving the Orin Line and heading east on the Black Hill Subdivision.

A Burlington Northern Santa Fe coal train powered by a trio of EMD SD70MACs, No. 9864 in 'Heritage II' colors and Nos 9563 and 9697 still in BN 'Grinstein' paint, heads south out of Donkey Creek on 29 May 1998.

Swinging through three curves, a loaded coal train approaches Donkey Creek on 29 May 1998. This early Burlington Northern Santa Fe train is powered by three Burlington Northern locomotives (GE C30-7, EMD SD40-2 and EMD SD60M) joined by a leased Oakway EMD SD60.

A northbound Burlington Northern Santa Fe coal train passes mile 14.5 on the Orin Subdivision at Caballo Junction on the morning of 30 May 1998.

A heard of cattle is definitely more interested in the photographer than the northbound BNSF coal train passing by in the background through Belle Ayr Junction on 30 May 2009.

Late in the day of 29 May 1998, a southbound Burlington Northern Santa Fe coal train crosses the bridge over Caballo Creek at milepost 17 on the Orin Line.

A southbound Union Pacific coal train approaches West Cordero Junction at a location once known as Haire on the Orin Subdivision in Powder River Basin on 30 June 2002.

In a view from the same spot as the photo above, the Union Pacific coal train is now passing by with a DPU (Distributed Power Unit) locomotive on the rear of the train. In the background is a portion of the Cordero Rojo coal mine complex.

Union Pacific and Burlington Northern Santa Fe coal empties wait to load at Cordero Junction on 7 June 2002. In the background are two trains on the Cordero Mine spur.

A BNSF coal empty charges through Coal Creek Junction on the morning of 14 June 2014. The tracks veering off the main line on the right is a 3.6-mile spur eastward to Coal Creek Mine.

Five Burlington Northern 7200-series EMD SD40-2s, along with a fuel tender, power a southbound coal train approaching Antelope on 26 July 1992. This portion of the Orin Line was still single track on this date, and Antelope was a siding south of Coal Creek Junction.

Heading north on the Orin Line at the old location of Antelope is a BNSF coal load led by GE ES44AC No. 5837 on 14 June 2014. Trackage here that was once single track with a siding is now three main tracks.

A southbound Burlington Northern coal train recedes in the distance moments after meeting a Chicago & North Western train at Antelope siding on 4 July 1989. Three C&NW EMD SD50s and a Union Pacific EMD SD60M power the northbound train.

A southbound Chicago & North Western coal load approaches Reno Junction, Wyoming, on 12 May 1995. The spring weather was getting stormy, and yes, it snowed the next day! Powering the train is C&NW GE AC4400CW No. 8808, Union Pacific EMD SD60M No. 6235, Norfolk Southern EMD SD70 No. 2519 and UP EMD SD60 No. 6035.

On 30 June 2002, a southbound Burlington Northern Santa Fe coal train passes a small homestead just north of Reno Junction.

A Union Pacific coal train passes the bungalow at 'MP 43.0' at Reno Junction on 30 May 2009. In the background, a train heads east on the spur out of Reno junction to either Black Thunder Mine or Black Thunder East Mine, while the actual loadout silo of Black Thunder West Mine can be seen on the left.

Three empty coal trains are staged on the Black Thunder Mine spur to be loaded at one of Black Thunder Mine's loadouts east of Reno Junction on the morning of 4 May 2007.

A northbound Chicago & North Western coal train meets a southbound Burlington Northern coal train at Reno Junction during a late snowfall on 13 May 1995. One of the crew members was on the train radio telling the opposing train how he already planted tomato plants in his garden, but should have waited a bit longer – springtime in Powder River Basin.

A southbound Union Pacific coal train crosses over from Track 3 to Track 1 at Crossover 45.7 south of Reno Junction on the damp morning of 14 June 2014.

A southbound Burlington Northern coal train crosses the bridge over Logan Draw and Antelope Creek just south of Naaco Junction on the morning of 26 July 1992. The Orin Subdivision was mostly single track at this point, and this draw would eventually be bridged by four main tracks, with four separate but adjoining bridges!

A loaded BNSF coal train powered by three EMD SD70ACes (one is on the rear of the train as DPU) approaches Converse Junction on 22 June 2018. The train will come to a stop in half a train length or so, to add two helper units on the rear for a trip up Logan Hill into Bill.

The BNSF train in the previous photo now has two Union Pacific pushers on the rear behind the BNSF EMD SD70ACe DPU locomotive and is helping it up Logan Hill at Converse Junction on 22 June 2018. In the foreground are two empties waiting to be loaded at Antelope Mine.

The multi-track Orin Subdivision main line through Converse Junction could frequently be a very busy stretch of railroad. On 29 June 2002, southbound Union Pacific coal trains meets on southbound BNSF, while a loaded train waits on the Antelope Mine spur in the foreground.

As a Chicago & North Western coal train loads at Antelope Mine, two other coal trains cruise through Converse Junction on 12 May 1995. A loaded C&NW coal train meets an empty Burlington Northern northbound with five SD40-2s splicing a fuel tender on the main.

A southbound BNSF coal train begins the climb up Logan Hill at Converse Junction on the afternoon of 21 June 2019. Fortunately, on the longest day of the year, there is no need for the weathered snow fences to break the progress of the drifting snow in the seemingly never-ending winds of Wyoming.

Tracks over Logan Hill in Powder River Basin are busy on the afternoon of 23 June 2018, as three Union Pacific coal trains cross this hill north of Bill.

After sunset at 9:00 p.m. on 2 July 2016, three Union Pacific coal trains converge on Logan Hill. On the right are DPUs of a load that has crested the hill and is headed south. On the next track over are two more DPUs of an empty headed back to a mine to load. Bright headlights of another load climbing the grade is led by SD70ACe No. 8753. A fourth train can be seen dropping down into Antelope Creek Valley in the middle background, its headlights distorted by hot exhaust.

Cactus are blooming among the grasses in Thunder Basin National Grasslands as a northbound Union Pacific coal train climbs Logan Hill north of Bill on 28 June 2015.

A southbound BNSF coal train approaches the Highway 59 overpass north of Bill on 21 June 2019. Coal tonnage on this portion of the Orin Line grew to the point that it justified four main tracks from Bill to Converse Junction over Logan Hill.

Just north of Bill, two Union Pacific coal trains meet under rolling clouds in a big Wyoming sky on the blustery morning of 4 May 2007.

A couple of horses relax as a southbound Union Pacific coal train arrives at Bill on 7 July 2005. Reportedly, the tiny 'town' of Bill got its name from a doctor that moved to the tiny settlement during the First World War, and that his wife came up with the town's name after noticing that several men in the area were all called Bill.

Five brand-new Chicago & North Western GE C44-9W locomotives line up with coal trains bound for loading in Powder River Basin at Bill on 7 July 1994.

Five Burlington Northern EMD SD40-2 spliced by a fuel tender take a northbound coal empty toward Bill for loading in Powder River Basin on 12 May 1995. BN used specially equipped tank cars as fuel tenders to extend the time between refueling for a locomotive set.

While cattle contently graze on a field lush with grass, a northbound Union Pacific coal empty crosses Box Creek south of Bill on the morning of 7 July 2005.

A Burlington Northern coal train heads south near Bill on 12 May 1995. With 12,000 hp of three EMD SD70MACs screaming above them, surprisingly the deer seem more interested in eating and in the photographer! BN SD70MACs were commonly called 'Grinsteins' after BN Chairman Gerald Grinstein, who was influential in the development of BN's final paint scheme.

An isolated morning thunderstorm dissipates and blows east as another Union Pacific coal train treads the busy rails of the Orin Line into Powder River Basin south of Bill on 30 May 2009.

Toward the end of another beautiful day in Wyoming, a southbound Burlington Northern Santa Fe coal train grinds past a oil well pump jack south of Bill on 8 July 1999.

On 4 July 1989, a northbound Burlington Northern coal train passes by the siding at Walker as it heads for a Powder River Basin coal mine. BN GE C30-7 No. 5037 leads a quartet of EMD SD40-2 locomotives, with a pair each of Union Pacific and BN, as power for the coal empty.

The sun is setting in Wyoming's Powder River Basin as a BNSF coal empty heads northbound south of Bill under a fiery western sky as the day ends on 29 May 2009.